AF433268

CONTENTS

INTRODUCTION

You have probably heard landscape designers speak of "hardscape," but the term, "softscape" is used less frequently. Intuitively, you may guess that being the opposite of hardscape, it must refer to everything in the landscape that is soft, but that would not be quite right. So let me furnish you with the precise definition.

Softscape comprises the animate (living), horticultural elements of landscape design. More simply put, it refers to the plants. Softscape elements are complemented by hardscape elements, such as wooden pergolas, stone walls, tile patios, and brick walkways.

Why is it incorrect to say that softscape simply means all the elements in one's landscaping that are soft? A tree is considered part of the softscape, but if you are playing catch with the kids in the yard and accidentally run full-steam into a tree's trunk, will it feel soft to you? Hardly, because you will most likely come away with a bruise. To qualify as softscape, an object has to be a plant. It does not have to be soft to the touch, although this will sometimes be the case. For example, velvety lamb's ear plants are as soft to the touch as possible.

WHAT IS SOFT SCAPING?

Softscape refers to the live horticultural elements of a landscape. Softscaping can include flowers, plants, shrubs, trees, co, and duties like weed/nuisance management, grading, planting, mowing, trimming, aerating, spraying, and digging for everything from plants and shrubs to flower beds. Wheel barrows and manual tools like rakes, shovels, picks, and gas power tools are commonly used.

Softscaping also refers to any duties involved with lawn care, such as planting, grading, mowing, fertilizing, trimming and digging. The purpose of softscape is to lend character to the landscaping, create an aura, ambience, and reflect the sensibilities of the inhabitants.

The term softscape stands in contrast to hardscape, which represents inanimate objects of a landscape such as pavers, stones, rocks, planter boxes, arbors, water feature as well as structures of wood and natural stone and concrete, like retaining walls, patios, fences and decks, pergolas, and stairs.

Live horticoltural elements include anything that is living, such as the following:

- Flowers
- Trees

- Shrubs
- Grass
- Flower Beds

Examples of softscape:

Remember, since "softscape" describes plant life, even a lawn grass (or common lawn weed, depending on your point of view) such as tall fescue grass counts. It is not just the showy plants that qualify. While a landscape designer would not normally include weedy plants under this heading, trying to exclude any class of plants is tricky because homeowners' tastes vary greatly. The philosopher, Emerson famously challenged our perception of what constitutes a "weed." Some gardeners go out of their way to grow beneficial weeds. But in offering examples of softscape below, we will stick to more conventional choices.

Most gardeners, even if they are just beginners, are familiar with annual plants. These are the plants displayed so prominently at garden centers in late spring, including the following red-white-and-blue trio popular in the U.S. around Memorial Day:

- Red salvia
- White alyssum
- Blue ageratum

The number of different kinds of perennials and biennials is mind-boggling. They grow in all sorts of different ways, inject great variety into the way your softscape looks, and serve all kinds of purposes.

For example, spring bulb plants, such as the Ambassador

allium in my picture, spring to life the next year from an underground bulb. Some perennials are quite tall. They are the kind of softscape you would grow up against a fence or wall in order to soften its appearance. Examples that come to mind are:

- Hollyhocks
- Delphiniums
- Foxglove

At the opposite end of the spectrum, some perennials are very short. The ones that spread furnish you with softscape potentially useful as a ground cover. Here are some ground covers of note:

- Creeping phlox
- Sweet woodruff
- Snow-in-summer

As showy as flower borders of annuals and perennials can be, trees, shrubs (bushes), and vines make perhaps the biggest softscape statements as individual plants:

- Golden chain trees
- Lilac bushes
- Hardy kiwi vines

When to Use Softscaping in your Landscaping Designs

Softscaping does an excellent job at accenting with your existing hardscape. Surrounding your walkways with flower beds and shrubs adds a nice touch to your property. In an earlier post, we discussed our Perennials are a great way to add colour to your landscape and require little to no maintenance other than the initial watering. A good mixture of hardscaping and softscaping brings a beautiful appearance to your home or office, as well as, increases both curb appeal and property value.

Does Sodding Qualify As Softscaping?

Reading through the definition above, sodding is most definitely considered softscape. Sodding directly involves fresh grass rolls, as well as, duties like digging, watering and grading. To learn more about sodding and how to get started with your own lawn, read the suggested material below.

How to Use Softscape

Many a reader interested in DIY landscape design has asked, How do you soften the straight edge of a patio? That is because, when given a choice, most people prefer a rounded edge on a hardscape feature, as opposed to a sharp, straight edge. A curve "flows" better and takes some of the "hard" out of hardscape (it is softer on the eyes).

There is a potential problem, though. Most people also prefer to make their lives easier rather than harder when undertaking a project. And building a brick patio with rounded edges is more difficult than building one with straight edges because you are working with a material (brick) that is rectangular. So you may have to make a choice between what looks better and what is easier to build.

- Softscape to the Rescue

In this article on building a brick patio, the emphasis was

placed on keeping the project as easy for beginners as possible. By using the basket weave brick pattern, we avoided having to cut bricks.

The drawback? You will end up with a square or rectangular patio in other words, one with straight edges. If you do not mind making your life a little more difficult, though, you can cut pavers and give your patio rounded edges, as long as you have the right equipment.

Is it possible to have your cake and eat it, too? It means complementing your hardscape with softscape. Specifically, what is referred to here as bringing in softscape is the use of container gardens along the straight edges of your patio to soften them.
For practical purposes, this method for softening sharp edges probably works best for small patios. A bigger patio means a longer edge, and a longer edge means that more container gardens will be required to achieve the softening effect. How much money are you willing to spend on softscape and containers?

Only you can answer that question, which is why we cannot put a number on it when, in that article, the statement is made that building bigger patios will require a different approach. While one can't quantify "bigger," the fact is that, after a patio reaches a certain size, the cost of having to soften the edges with softscape becomes prohibitive. In such cases, it is probably best to use a curved hardscape design if you want to avoid straight edges.

COMMON SOFTSCAPE COMPONENTS

Consider these the "soft" horticultural (living, growing) components of the landscape. These might include flowers, trees, shrubs, ground covers, etc. Change and evolve constantly, as they grow and adapt to climate and other conditions.

Are softer to the touch, quite literally. Think about touching the leaves of a tree or perennial, or blades of grass. They are soft, not hard. Suitable soil conditions are vital for the development of any plant. When it comes to landscape design, understanding the different kinds of soil that are suitable for different kinds of plants is non-negotiable. This is especially true if your lawn seeks to en-mesh nature with hardscape elements.

When you've spent so much energy, effort, and time making sure that your outdoor living space looks incredible and inviting, you also want to ensure that it remains in pristine condition. And that won't happen unless you take care of all the plants, shrubs, flowers, or berries that you've planted.

Some gardening enthusiasts claim that plants can grow in

any kind of soil. This is partially true, but for a plant to grow up to its optimal state and under the best circumstances, soil management is important.

In a well-planned landscape, elements should be positioned so they look attractive and are primed for continued growth and health. The climate, type of soil, amount of light, and drainage conditions are all things to consider when planning softscapes, the natural, living features of a landscape, including trees, bushes, flowers, and other plants. Common softscape components include:

Trees, shrubs, and ground cover. Use trees, shrubs, and various types of ground cover to create visually rich, aesthetically pleasing designs. As you select plants for your landscape, consider species of trees and shrubs that are native to the area.

- Flower gardens.

Many homeowners incorporate both perennials and annuals into the garden design to ensure a varying palette of color throughout the year. For example, tulips are annuals that are often planted in the late fall for color throughout the winter months. When the tulips are done blooming, summer annuals replace them.

- Mulch.

For unused sections of the yard, low-maintenance options like mulch may be preferred over grass. Mulch helps pre-

vent weed growth and provides an insulating layer that holds heat and moisture in the soil. Because mulch decomposes, it typically needs to be replenished once or twice a year.

Other Components of Softscape

- Establishing beds and borders
- Improving soil (Topsoil)
- Laying turf or improving turf
- Choosing, planting or moving trees
- Choosing, planting or moving shrubs
- Planting and maintaining hedges
- Creating planting themes
- Pruning
- Container planting
- Creating a vegetable plot
- Outdoor lighting

Preparing a New Bed or Border

Creating a new bed or border is a bit like decorating a room in the house. You have an idea of what it might look like, but there is a fair bit of work to do before you achieve a finished result. The secret of success is not to cut corners but prepare properly, choose your plants wisely and take your time. A hurried job rarely produces the best results.

- Straight or curved?

It may seem obvious to lay out the borders in your garden to follow the fence line. However that accentuates the shape of the garden, defining the boundaries, rather thanNew border making your plot more interesting. Gently curved borders, deeper in the corners, soften the edges and can make the space look larger. Simple sweeping curves are best. Avoid wavy edges, they look contrived and fussy and are difficult to maintain. Straight borders, which create strong angles, can look effective, especially in small gardens if you want a more formal or contemporary effect.

- Make those borders wide enough

Whichever you choose, make your borders wide enough. A narrow border along a boundary is useless, unless you just want to grow climbing plants. Even then it is best to plant them at least 30cm (1ft) away from a wall or fence. Wider borders are easier to manage, because they give your plants the space to grow and you will not have to keep cutting them back to contain them in the space.

It is better to have fewer planting areas, but make them bigger. One metre wide is really a minimum, two metres better. Just go out and measure the width of a single shrub, rose bush, or perennial and you will see how much space is needed. It is particularly important to have enough space in a bed or border where you want to plant larger shrubs or trees, perhaps to screen a neighbouring property, or just as a backdrop to your garden.

- Removing the turf

Wide borderIf the area of your new bed or border is covered in grass, then the first job is to remove it. In most cases this is best done manually, rather than using a weedkiller. When you have marked out the planting area cut around it using a sharp spade, pushed into the ground vertically to the depth of a few centimetres. If you are unsure about the line, be conservative. It is easy to take away more grass, but much harder to put it back. Then remove spade-width strips of grass by cutting around them and slipping the spade under them just beneath the soil surface. These can be stacked face down in a corner of the garden and allowed to rot. They will produce some nice, loamy soil for use later.

- Get rid of the weeds

If there are any perennial weeds, you must tackle those before you start planting. Bindweed, thistles, ground elder, nettles and other perennial weeds will re-emerge fromSBK Brushwood Killer root fragments you leave in the soil as you dig. If you have light, sandy soil it may be possible to dig them out carefully, but in most cases it will be necessary to use a weedkiller.

Effective herbicides that control perennial weeds without permanently damaging the ground do not work on bare soil. They must be applied to weeds in growth. So allow them to develop plenty of leaves, then treat with SBK Tough Weedkiller. This gets right down to kill the roots and will kill even woody weeds, but not grass. It takes time to work and may mean you have to delay planting; you must not replant for six weeks after application anyway. If the weed problem is serious it will be worth it.

- Conditioning the soil

When the ground is clean, fork it over thoroughly to a depth greater than the head of a digging fork. You may prefer to use a spade. If the soil is heavy a border spade is easier and lighter to use. Next add plenty of organic matter; this improves the texture of the soil. It makes it easier to cultivate and it helps your plants' roots to penetrate the soil and get established. Soils that are rich in organic matter are better at hanging on to water and nutrients, therefore plants grow more successfully.

Organic manure is a great way to condition soil without the need to add vast quantities of bulky organic matter. It's light and easy to handle and perfect to boost fertility and improve soil texture. For best results rough dig the soil leaving it in large clods, apply organic Manure, leave for a few days and then fork it over.

If the soil is incredibly sticky, in other words clay, or very compacted you will get better results by applying Clay Breaker. This breaks up that sticky mass into crumbs that are easier to cultivate. The Clay Breaker granules are easy to apply over roughly dug ground at any time of the year, however autumn and winter is the ideal time; preparing the ground ready for planting in spring.

Improve Your Topsoil

- Adding Nutrients and Improving Soil Structure

If you are passionate about your garden, it will be important to you that you maintain the quality of your topsoil. Everyone has their own tried and tested methods or opinions of what you can do, but at the end of the day, the measures you should take depend entirely on your soil type.

- Testing Your Soil Type

There is a very simple test to help you determine your soil type, called the sausage test, or the ribbon test. Simply take a handful of soil from the garden, add water, then squeeze out the excess liquid. Roll your soil into the shape of a sausage, then try and bend your soil sausage into a circular shape.

If the soil keeps it shape for a while, your soil has higher clay content. However, if your soil breaks up quickly, it has a higher sand content. Alternatively, purchase a kit which contains detailed instructions, and then send your sample away for analysis. Once you have established the kind of soil in your garden (some areas may find their soil is a combination), you can begin to look at how you can improve your soil.

- Improving Clay Soil

Clay soil is heavier and chunky, and it needs to be broken down as it does not drain very well. One way you can break it up is by raking it with manure.

This helps with drainage by 'opening up' the soil, while also fertilising the soil in the process. Some gardeners prefer to use gypsum or, in the case of acidic soils, dolomite (calcium and magnesium).

- Improving Sandy Soil

Sandy soil is pretty much the opposite of clay soil: it repels water and will not hold water well, if at all. It should be tackled because it will lose all the nutrition and water you put into it until it has been improved.

Organic soil improvers are the best place to start. Sheep manure is easy to apply, but using a mulch will also help. Mulches lie on top, gradually breaking down into the soil, and they will help to hold moisture, fertilise your soil and maintain a stable temperature. An added bonus with mulches is the role they play in preventing and reducing weed growth. You might find you need to add an extra layer now and again as your mulch breaks down.

- Adding Nutrients to Your Soil

There are many other ways to improve quality and add nutrition to your topsoil. Among the most popular choices are:

- Leaf mould :excellent for adding nutrients and also improves drainage, but it can be difficult to collect enough so it is often used with other soil improvers.
- Seaweed mulch: a black soil-like mix that looks great but also contains almost everything that plants need to thrive. May need to be covered by bark mulch in dry areas to prevent evaporation.

How To Lay Turf

- Measuring and Ordering

Laying instant turf requires accurate measurements. Use a tape measure to work out the area of your planned lawn, include these measurements on a sketch of the lawn area with the length and width and any unusual features. As professional instant lawn suppliers, we can determine the amount of instant turf you will need from your sketch.

If the area is of a rectangular shape, then all you need do is phone the measurements through and we will work it out for you. Please measure your turf area carefully as we are unable to accept returns following a new lawn installation.

Schedule your order for delivery of turf after preparatory work is completed and you are ready to for your new lawn installation. A key turf installation tip is to laying turf promptly on the day of delivery to ensure a strong beginning and healthy foundation. Knowing how to lay grass effectively can make a big difference in the longevity and enjoyment of your lawn.

- Soil Preparation

When planning how to lay instant turf on your property, proper soil preparation is essential. For best results, use a lawn rotary hoe or dig the area evenly to a depth of 100mm to 150mm. Eliminate drainage problems for your instant turf in Melbourne by having soil slope away from the house etc.

Check to see that your soil does not require lime, if it does, apply at the recommended dose, then rake in a complete lawn starter fertilizer to optimize. Rake and smooth the soil removing any rocks, roots and large clods. Roll and consolidate the soil lightly, this will firm the soil surface and reveal any low areas that need more soil. Keep the soil level 20mm below paths etc. Water the prepared area to settle the soil and provide a moist base for the turf.

- Turf Installation

Install your lawn immediately upon delivery by rolling out your instant turf. Turf is a living plant that requires ground contact and moisture to survive. In hot weather, protect unlaid turf by placing stacks in shade, or lightly sprinkling with water. Begin installing turf along the longest straight line such as a driveway or path.

Butt and push edges and ends against each other tightly, without stretching. Avoid gaps or over lapping. Stagger the joints in each row in a brick like fashion, using a large knife to trim corners etc. Avoid leaving small strips at outer edges as they will not retain moisture. On slopes place turf across the slope.

Rolling turf after laying is important. After installing the turf, roll the lawn with a lawn roller to improve turf to soil contact and remove air pockets.

Following installation and until it is established, you should avoid walking or kneeling on the new turf as this will cause indentations or air pockets.

- Turf Watering

Instant turf in Melbourne and Australia-wide must be watered within half an hour of laying instant grass.

Regardless of the weather, give your new lawn installation least 25mm (1") of water within half an hour of laying. Water daily or more often, keeping turf moist until it is firmly rooted (about 2 weeks). These first two weeks are the most critical time for the turf. Do not all Turf to dry out. Establishment of new turf can take up to 2 months in the cooler months.

After two weeks, regular and deeper watering should begin. Weather conditions will dictate the amount and frequency of watering. Be certain that your new lawn has enough moisture to survive hot, dry or windy periods. An important turf installation tip is to water areas near buildings more often where reflected heat dries the turf.

Caution: During the first three weeks avoid heavy or concentrated use of your new lawn to ensure your new lawn installation can firmly knit with soil for a successful, smooth turf.

Turf Maintenance

- Mowing

Regular mowing with either a rotary or cylinder type mower is essential for your instant turf in Melbourne and Victoria. Your new instant lawn should be mown 10-14 days after installation. Continue to mow often, generally no more than 1/3 of the grass height at a mowing. Keep your mower blades sharp. For correct cutting heights refer to the Instant Turf page.

- Fertilizing

Fertilizer should be applied on a regular basis all year round. Our professional lawn supply team can advise which fertiliser will suit your instant turf type and budget. Small applications at frequent intervals give the best results.

For example, 1 ½kg/100m2 per month of lawn fertilizer will keep your new lawn in an active healthy condition. From time to time you may need advice or assistance in caring for your lawn. Contact us directly for the best lawn care advice possible.

 Keep in mind that your new lawn increases your property value significantly. With proper care it will remain a great asset, providing beauty, a clean playing surface and an improved environment for many years.

Tips for Laying Turf

- Consider when to lay the turf: It is best to lay turf in the non-winter months. Ensure that the turf is not used for a few weeks after installation so that it can establish well.
- Consider where to lay the turf: Think about where you are going to lay the turf including the location, surrounding environment, access to water and the quality of the soil.
- Research grass types: Different grass types have different characteristics, and some are better suited to certain environments over others. Ask a professional and conduct online research.
- Choose a suitable grass type: Choose turf that

is best suited to your requirements and needs. For example, consider maintenance, usage, shade tolerance, water tolerance and weed and pest resistance.

- Assess the quality of your soil: At Anco Turf we provide a free soil test. Bring in kilogram of soil and we will conduct a ph test and to you know whether it is ideal.
- Add nutrients to your soil: A sandy soil is ideal. Consider adding nutrients to the soil to enhance its vitality and to prep it well for fresh grass.
- Measure turf area: At Anco Turf we have a handy turf calculator that will help you calculate linear shapes. Input the dimensions in metres, and the area will be calculated automatically. Always add 5% to each dimension to be safe.
- Prepare the underlay: Before you install the lawn, remember to prepare the underlay by killing off existing vegetation, ensuring a sandy soil base, adding nutrients, and smoothening and levelling the surface.
- Lay the turf: Remember to spray fertiliser before installation. Immediately after delivery of fresh turf, install it by unravelling the rolls carefully. Start in one corner and work your way to the diagonally opposite corner.
- Maintenance following installation: For a period of at least 6 weeks following installation, you will need to water every day. Keep traffic to a minimum. The first mow should be at a higher than usual setting to avoid shock. Add fertiliser after the first 6 weeks.

Transplanting or Moving Trees and Shrubs in the Landscape

The best way to avoid these moments is to plan from the start. Before planting anything, we suggest you try to take a look into the future of your landscape and install plants that fit your future needs. Are you planning to build an addition onto your home? Will your recreational activities change in the future? How big will that adorable tree or shrub you just brought home from the garden center get when it reaches maturity?

Sometimes, no matter how carefully you planned, a large tree or shrub needs to be removed from its current location. If you decide to try to relocate these plants, first consider hiring a professional with the equipment and knowledge to do the job. Digging and moving trees can be a difficult and very heavy proposition and is not a job for people who have health problems, back conditions, or are out of shape.

To choose a professional, get estimates from at least three companies. Request references for their work and information about their credentials and insurance. Ask for an explanation of how they will prepare and move the plant, as well as instructions on the post-transplanting care you need to provide.

- Site Evaluation

To increase your chances of success, evaluate the suitability of the new planting site by checking the growing conditions, including light levels, soil pH, drainage, and exposure. In other words, assume you are selecting a new plant for the new site and ask the question "do the conditions at the site meet the growing requirements of the plant?" If it does not appear that your plant will survive and thrive in that site you should reconsider moving it there.

- Root Pruning

Transplanting established trees and shrubs is somewhat risky because you will damage many of the feeder roots during the transplanting process. Feeder roots are responsible for absorbing the majority of essential nutrients and water. To minimize the shock to the plant, we recommend root pruning several months to one year in advance of the move, depending on the size and type of the plant.

Pruning the roots will encourage the plant to produce a flush of new feeder roots. The goal is to allow the plant to develop new feeder roots within the zone of the future root ball that will be moved. This will reduce the amount of transplant shock the plant experiences. Before root pruning you should consider the size of the root ball that will be moved.

The greater the root ball diameter, the more roots will be included in the move. Also remember that bigger root balls weigh more. Consider how the plant will be lifted and moved. Ball carts, wagons, tarps, or thick folded cardboard can be helpful in transporting the dug plant to its new location.

When to root prune depends on when you wish to move the plant. For most plants, root pruning is recommended in the fall, followed by transplanting in the spring. This allows the plant to grow new feeder roots in the pruned zone over the winter without the burden of supporting new growth. For larger plants, you may want to root prune one year or more before transplanting. Keep in mind larger plants will need more time to become established after transplanting.

Alternatively, rooting pruning in the spring for a fall move is possible; however, the root pruned plant will need to be watered during summer dry spells. Be aware some plants do not respond well to being moved in the fall, especially those with thick and fleshy roots (e.g., Magnolia, tulip poplar, oaks, birch, rhododendrons, hemlocks, and flowering dogwood).

Methods for root pruning vary. One method called spading involves cutting through the existing roots with a spade, making a circular cut all the way around the plant. The edge of this cut should be just inside the edge of the future root ball. Spading works best for small plants or plants that have not been in the old site for a long time.

Another method called trenching involves digging a trench around the plant and refilling the trench where the new feeder roots with develop with soil high in organic matter. Trenching is more appropriate for plants that have been located in the old site for several years or more. Trenching techniques also vary, depending on plant size. Trenching can be done all the way around the plant or only part of the way around the plant, followed by further trenching later in the season. To root prune using trenching, dig a trench 8 to 12 inches wide or wider, 12 inches deeper or deeper with the outer edge of the trench corresponding to the outer edge of the future root ball.

Next, fill the trench with soil high in organic matter, made by mixing two parts topsoil with one part compost. If conditions are good, the plant will grow new feeder roots in the trench of rich soil by transplanting time.

These feeder roots will give the tree added ability to withstand transplant shock. Be sure to move as many of these new, young roots as you can when you move the plant. Before digging the root ball for transplanting, check to see if a good net of fibrous roots has developed. If few roots are found in the trench, you should consider postponing the move for another year. In addition, when you do decide to move the plant, digging a root ball larger than originally planned may assure that all of the new roots go with it.

Once the roots are pruned, special care should be taken to assure the root ball receives sufficient moisture, especially in the event of a dry fall or winter season. Check for soil moisture levels by feeling the soil. If the soil is dry two to three inches below the surface, give the tree a good soaking, assuring that the trench area is well watered. A two to three inch layer of mulch over the root ball but not in contact with the trunk or stems of the plant can help hold moisture in the soil and also protect the roots from cold temperatures during the winter.

- Transplanting

Prior to moving the plant, prepare and dig the hole for the plant in the new location. Also soak the root ball of the plant before moving so that the soil will remain together during the digging process. Carefully dig the soil away from the root ball, and then wrap the whole ball in untreated natural burlap. Be very careful not to use synthetic burlap because it will not rot away and will eventually restrict the growth of the roots. Lash the burlap together securely to hold the roots firmly in place. You can do this by using a large upholstery needle and untreated natural twine to stitch the burlap tightly around the root ball.

Carefully move the plant using a cart, a rented ball cart, burlap, or cardboard. The goal is to keep the root ball intact. If the soil ball breaks, it will break the roots inside and may lead to the death of the plant. Make sure the plant is set at the same depth in the new hole and fill in around the root ball with topsoil. Mulch lightly with three to four inches of mulch, keeping the mulch off of the trunk or stems of the plant, and be sure to provide adequate water throughout the entire next growing season.

How to Plant Hedges

- Prepare the soil for planting

You can skip your arm workout today digging up the soil for your hedge will be more than enough exertion! The depth and breadth of the ditch you dig should be based on the roots of your plant, i.e. it should be around 1.5 times bigger than the roots. To ensure the hedge grows straight, put a piece of string around the area you want to dig up.

To make your hedge as thick and dense as possible, it's best to plant three to four plants per metre. So get your shovel and start digging. Once you've finished, loosen up the earth at the bottom a little this will give the roots more room to spread out.

- Give your plants a new home

Once you've finished digging your ditch and have loosened up the earth, it's time to put your plants in the soil. They will probably come in either burlap cloth (to protect the roots) or in a plastic container. If burlap cloth is wrapped around the roots, you can leave the plants in it when you insert them into the ditch. Then untie the cloth, fold down the sides and bury it in the soil. To prevent the root balls from falling apart, the plants should not be moved again. Cover two-thirds of the roots with soil and water. Then insert the rest of the soil and carefully even it out with your foot to ensure the earth is well anchored. If your plants are in plastic containers, remove them before putting them into the ditch, then water them well and cover them with earth.

- Spray

Once you've planted your hedge, you need to take good care of it. If you want a beautiful hedge, you need to be attentive. This means one thing above all: watering it. To begin with, every three to four days is a good rule of thumb. Over time, you can probably increase the periods between watering. Your plants should get 10 litres of water for every metre in height. Of course, the exact amount of water they need also depends on the soil and type of plant but this rule will enable you to make a rough estimate. So, if your hedge plants are half a metre high, approx. five litres of water per plant should suffice.

For older hedges, regular watering is no longer necessary because of their deep roots, and you should only need to water them during long dry spells. If you can get in the habit of watering your hedge in the morning, you'll be doing both yourself and your plants a favour. The soil is cooler in the morning, so the water doesn't evaporate and can really reach the roots. When watering, direct the water stream right at the soil. The leaves will then take what they need from the earth. Watering the leaves directly could have an adverse effect and potentially encourage fungus diseases.

- Fertilise your hedge

You can help your hedge to grow by fertilising it in the spring and/or in the autumn. In most cases, it's enough to add a little mature compost at the foot of the plant. Simply sprinkle it on the soil and rake it a little. For deciduous hedges and those with rotting leaves, such as privet, you can also use the leftover foliage and branches from trimming as fertiliser. After trimming, simply rake a little foliage into the soil beneath the hedge. More demanding plants such as rhododendron need acidic soil. To create this environment, you can add peat to the earth. You can also use horn shavings for fertiliser.

- Trim your hedge like a pro

A hedge is a bit like human hair: to help it grow and look good, you need to cut it from time to time. Depending on the condition and age of your hedge, it may be a question of simple maintenance or shaping, or moderate to radical pruning. Whatever your aim, it's easiest with a pair of electric hedgecutters. For each cutting technique you want to try, you should select the appropriate teeth spacing (the distance between the individual teeth on the cutter blade).

The right trimming technique is crucial. Picture of someone cutting a hedge with a Bosch hedgecutter .Trimming helps to stimulate growth and keep your hedge in shape

Types of Prunning
- Light pruning

You should give non-deciduous (evergreen) hedges a light prune once a year, ideally between May and August. Deciduous hedges should ideally be trimmed twice a year, once in spring and once in late summer/early autumn. It's best to wait until the main bud break to do the second trim, when the newly grown buds are fully developed and the hedge isn't growing quite as much. That way the cut will last a little longer. Dry, overcast and frost-free days are ideal for trimming work; strong, direct sunlight could damage the shoots.

For contouring and light pruning, a pair of cutters with a small teeth spacing is sufficient because you're mainly cutting young, thin branches. Ideally, you should trim your hedge in a trapezoid shape, i.e. the bottom branches should be longer than the top ones to ensure that all parts of the hedge get plenty of light. You can clip approx. 10–15 cm of the newly grown shoots straight across. To make sure the hedge isn't crooked, you can again use a piece of string to guide you.

- Moderate pruning

for this type of trim, you should make sure that the teeth spacing on your cutters is bigger than the thickness of the branches. It's best to work on frost-free days and cut back the fruit-bearing branches by as much as two-thirds. By doing so, you can remove the competing shoots, so the branches can again sprout buds effectively. For hedge plants that stem from trees, such as the field maple or hornbeam, you can prune three-quarters of the shoot tips in the first year. This will help the branches grow more widely/densely and make for a thicker hedge.

- Hard pruning

sometimes, older hedges need more radical pruning to restore their glory days and close over any gaps. Frost-free winter days are perfect for this type of work. It's best to use cutters with a large teeth spacing and a powerful motor. Prune back the branches to the thickest trunk and they will grow back more densely in the spring.

Outdoor lighting

- Smart Outdoor Lights

Outdoor lights for entryways, porches, and landscapes that you can control using an app installed on your mobile device give you more control over how you light a landscape.

- Stairway Lights

Riser lights, under-tread lights, recessed wall fixtures, and pathway lights all can be used to illuminate outdoor stairways. "By day, the best stairway lighting is barely noticeable. After the sun goes down, well chosen lights can transform staircases to glowing jewel boxes.

- Porch Lights

A covered porch offers protection from the elements. Be sure to get a light rated for damp conditions but consider this an opportunity to add personality and curb appeal to your home. For more porch light ideas.

- Solar Lights

Solar lights are powered by light from the sun, and have three essential three parts: a photovoltaic solar panel, a rechargeable battery, and an led lamp. The solar panel harnesses energy from the sun during the day time and stores this energy in a battery.

Usually, solar lamps come with sensors to automatically turn on the led light when energy from the sun is no longer available. The stored energy in the battery lights up the lamp.

LANDSCAPE DESIGN

- Composition Of The Soil

You'll also need to know the composition of soil to get to know why each type is different. Every kind consists of mineral particles in three different compositions. Sand is the dominant particle, followed by silt, and then clay. The amount of each particle in the soil decides its texture and various other properties.

The following are the kinds of soil that are most suitable for landscape designs:

- Clay soil: This kind of soil has dense but tiny particles that play a huge role in retaining nutrients and moisture. The downside of choosing clay soil is that it becomes hard and compact when left to dry which means it needs continuous moisture.

- Sandy soil: This is the exact opposite of clay soil. Sandy soil has large particles, allowing the water and nutrients to move easily.

- Silts: This soil has finer particles that are compactly packed together. This improves air circulation and drainage within the soil.

- Loam: This is the ideal kind of soil for most plants.

It has the perfect balance of all three particles (sand, silt and clay).

Why Is Soil Management Important For Landscape Design?

Plants have varying needs and respond differently to the same environment. Soil varies in texture, quality, and depth throughout your lawn. It can be starkly different from one patch to another, even within the same property.

Learning about soil management before a landscaping project is important because it will keep your outdoor space in shape.

Soil is a storehouse for nutrients; it comprises organic matter, microorganisms, minerals, air, and water. The mineral part is made of small rocks that disintegrated over time. The organic portion, on the other hand, consists of animal and plant ruminants that are at different levels in the decomposition process.

CONCLUSION

As a quick summary to the above post, softscaping refers to anything that directly involves any live horticultural elements of a landscape and any duties/services (weed removal) that goes with it. It can be used effectively with hardscaping (interlocking, walkways, stones) to add a beautiful contrast to your landscape or property.